Box Turtle

Children's Book: An Amazing Animal Picture Book about Box Turtle for Kids

By

Elena Fabio

Elena Fabio

I am a box turtle.

I look like a small box because of my shell.

I can hide my head and feet inside my shell.

I have an upward hooked jaw that looks like a beak.

The colors on my shell are mostly brown and yellow.

I am small.

I am fragile.

I am shy and most of the time, I hide inside my shell.

I have many brothers and sisters; we hatched almost at the same time.

I am a cute looking creature.

I am quiet and I don't make too much sound.

I rarely get out and travel.

I often stay in moist wooded areas.

I am easily stressed.

I need sunlight to stay healthy.

I am a great pet.

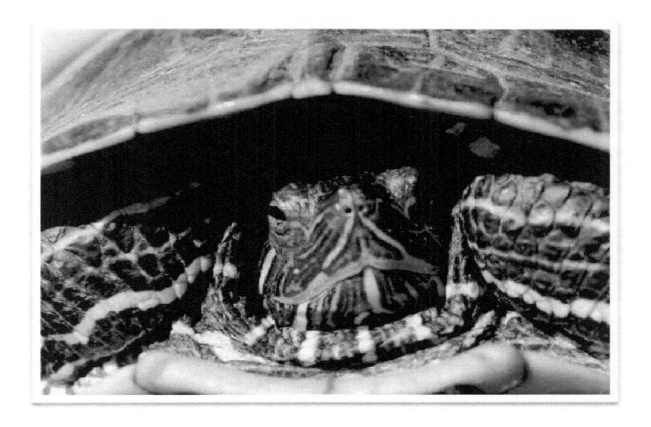

I eat small insects and plants.

When I am lost, I aimlessly try to find my way back home.

I am very slow.

I lay eggs just like the birds, even if I am not a bird.

I can lay many eggs at once.

I can live up to 100 years old just like humans.